D0388888

AVE MARIA

AVE MARIA

The Mystery of a Most Beloved Prayer

POPE FRANCIS

A Conversation with Marco Pozza

Translated from the Italian by Matthew Sherry

IMAGE

NEW YORK

Copyright © 2018 by Rizzoli Libri, S.p.A., Rizzoli, Milano

Copyright © 2018 by Libreria Editrice Vaticana,
Citta del Vaticano
Translation copyright © 2019 by Penguin Random House LLC

All rights reserved.
Published in the United States by Image,
an imprint of the Crown Publishing Group, a division
of Penguin Random House LLC, New York.
ImageCatholicBooks.com

IMAGE is a registered trademark and the "I" colophon
is a trademark of Penguin Random House LLC.

Originally published in Italy as AVE MARIA: IL SANTO
PADRE CI RACCONTA IL MISTERO DI MARIA CON LE PAROLE
DELLA PREGHIERA PIÙ AMATA by Rizzoli Libri, S.p.A.,
Milan, in 2018.

Library of Congress Cataloging-in-Publication data is
available upon request.

ISBN 978-1-9848-2650-3
Ebook ISBN 978-1-9848-2651-0

PRINTED IN THE UNITED STATES OF AMERICA

Book design: Elizabeth Rendfleisch
Jacket design: Sarah Horgan
Front jacket image: Madonna at Prayer (oil on canvas),
Il Sassoferrato (Giovanni Battista Salvi)/Bridgeman Images

10 9 8 7 6 5 4 3 2 1

First U.S. Edition

Contents

Contents

Part II

A Note to Readers

Hail Mary, full of Grace, the Lord is with thee.

Mysteries engage our senses and our intellect. They challenge us to solve a puzzle or pay attention to people, places, or situations we may normally overlook. That is why we can call the Blessed Virgin Mary and her prayer the Ave Maria grand mysteries, because both call us to pause, look, and listen to how we live our lives and how we respond to the often mystifying callings of God. Both Mary and the prayer that honors her stimulate us and bring new life to our hearts and our imagination in ways that challenge and deepen our faith.

It is with great reverence that Image Books is publishing *Ave Maria: The Mystery of a Most Beloved Prayer* by Pope Francis, a follow-up to his 2018 book *Our Father: Reflections on the Lord's Prayer.* Pope Francis has a deep devotion to Mary, and his love for our Heavenly Mother is demonstrated on every page that follows.

As with *Our Father*, this book is a conversation with Father Marco Pozza, a priest and prison chaplain from Padua, Italy, and is supplemented with some of Pope Francis's most attentive and heartfelt meditations on Mary, her role in Jesus's life, and the need for all of us to follow her example of loyalty and service. Certain adjustments to the original Italian texts, including colloquialisms, punctuation, and grammar, have been made for the sake of cohesion and consistency.

Blessings,
Gary Jansen, Director of Image Books
March 5, 2019

Pure Hope

In the death and resurrection of Jesus, God the Father has inaugurated the new creation, a way of living *by the standard of God*. As the apostle Paul says, Jesus "is our peace, he who made both one and broke down the dividing wall of enmity, through his flesh" (Eph 2:14).

For all of us who belong to different cultures, traditions, histories, this opens up the concrete possibility of truly becoming one, *like* the Father, the Son, and the Holy Spirit. That is what the Church is—the holy faithful people of God, the family of the children of God. The leader of this work of reconciliation and unity is the Holy Spirit, who always creates relationships, builds bridges, strengthens bonds, consoles in sorrow, and gives the strength and joy of forgiveness and mercy.

The Holy Spirit is in fact the one who ceaselessly,

day and night, pours into our hearts the love of the Father (cf. Rm 5:5) and thus helps us to become more and more the children of God, true brothers and sisters among ourselves.

In this way our vocation, the great gift that the Father has given to us, is that of allowing ourselves, even though we are poor, lowly, ordinary human beings, to resemble Christ, to participate in his life and his joy. Jesus is our big brother, the new man, the true man; and in him we too as children finally begin to resemble our Father and to resemble one another.

The Church is thus the community of those who have been offered the possibility of being new men and women, clothed in the Spirit, men and women whose hearts resemble that of Christ: the complete gift of self and unconditional acceptance of every other person.

This possibility is for all of us a journey, often rough, grueling, made up of setbacks and breakthroughs, in which the light of God's love is still hidden by the veil of our poverty, our meager faith, our lack of love. And indeed *by the gift* of the Father, we are already truly his children; however, our resemblance to him is not yet realized, and at times seems to be nothing but an illusion. All of this requires a great deal of patience, with ourselves and with others, a patience as great as that of the Holy Spirit. As an author once wrote, the Holy Spirit is precisely *the master of slow maturations.*

All of this can give rise in us to the great temptation of discouragement, because in spite of our many gifts . . . we are truly *a stiff-necked people* (cf. Ex 33:3, 34:9).

In the face of this risk of discouragement, then, the Father has given us a presence of *pure hope,* a firm foothold, a certainty that what he is bringing about in us is effective if it is welcomed with faith and cooperation, even though the results so far may not seem to mean much.

Mary is in fact this masterpiece of the Father, the one who is "full of grace" (cf. Lk 1:28). In her we see the result of God's action, meaning she is the example of what happens to a human being who welcomes the Holy Spirit completely. The person becomes a splendor of goodness, of love, of beauty, one who is "blessed among women" (cf. Lk 1:42). The Lord Jesus, dying on the cross, gave us Mary as our Mother, precisely because she is his real Mother and he has really become our brother. So that in Mary, Mother of God, Mother of the Risen One, of all of us who rise again in him in baptism, we see the result of God's work in humanity. Mary is the masterpiece that the Lord seeks to realize and is realizing with his infinite patience in the Church, in every one of us and in the holy people of God in its entirety.

Mary is thus the universal Mother who gives total attention, care, closeness to each son, to each daughter. In her we see in fact the heart of a woman that beats *like* that of God, a heart that beats for all, without distinction. She is truly the human face of God's infinite goodness.

Mary is the Mother of Jesus, the God-man. In her Son she encounters both God and man; when she speaks with him, she is addressing both God and man. So in her we see that it is really true that loving the Lord means truly loving humanity, and vice versa. And so, when we are looking at her, Mary constantly helps us and teaches us to turn to the Lord. When Mary realizes that the wine for their friends' wedding banquet in Cana has run out, she does not take the initiative to find the solution, saying, "Now I'll take care of this; go do this and that . . ." No, on the contrary, she always points to her Son, and suggests to the servants: "Do whatever he tells you" (Jn 2:5).

This is why Christians have always turned to her as their refuge, as the one who always points the way to the Lord and invites us to entrust to him unconditionally the people dearest to us, the most delicate problems, the most convoluted situations. When it seems there is no way out, Mary is "our hope," because—as Dante said (cf. *Paradiso* 33, 14–15)—if one wants a grace and does not turn to Mary, one is like a bird that wants to fly without wings.

After the experience of spiritual dialogue last year with Fr. Marco Pozza on the *Our Father,* I thought it would be a good idea to discuss with him another prayer that accompanies all of us throughout our lives. The *Hail Mary* is taught to us when we are little, and even if it is neglected it comes right back to our lips during times of difficulty in particular, but above all it reemerges in our hearts.

Saint Cyprian of Carthage, a bishop and martyr of the third-century Church, said that no one can have God as Father if he does not have the Church as Mother (*On the Unity of the Catholic Church* 6). And in Mary we see the most beautiful face of the Church-Mother; we see the dream that the Lord has for each one of us and the hope that dwells within us, in spite of the fact that our hearts are still full of contradictions. And thus Mary, while accompanying us and revealing to us how good the Lord is (cf. 1 Pt 2:3), restores our courage. Her greatest desire is to lead all of us to the Father; thus, although we are often still divided among ourselves, we can truly become one family in Jesus, her Son and our Lord, King of mercy and head of the Body that is the Church.

God is our Father, and in Mary the Church shows us her most splendid motherly face.

Franciscus

Part I

Hail, Mary, full of grace,
the Lord is with you.
Blessed are you among women
and blessed is the fruit of your womb, Jesus.
Holy Mary, Mother of God,
pray for us sinners,
now and at the hour of our death.

Amen.

Hail, Mary, Full of Grace

Pope Francis, Mary has been painted, sculpted, and re-counted. She is one of the most desired, most feared, and also most studied figures. Mary has been defended by the popes and is often the one most sought after by sinners. She is the one most hated by Lucifer. But only the Lord was able to win her over with a greeting that has no equal: "Hail, Mary, full of grace" (cf. Lk 1:28). No creature has ever been able to boast of such a greeting from heaven. So when I recite the Hail Mary *I am moved, because it seems to me that I am listening to the beginning of the history that changed humanity's fate. A proclamation of mercy: it is like saying that God is starting over, and starting over with a woman. It is touching to know that Christianity begins like this.*

God greets a woman with a great truth: "I have made you full of my love, full of myself, and just as you will be full of myself, you will be full of my Son, and then of all the children of the Church." But the grace does not end there. The beauty of Our Lady is a beauty that bears fruit, a beauty that is mother. Let's not forget it: God greets a woman who is mother from the first moment, is already presented as mother at the very moment in which she conceives.

It is curious that Mary's biography should be enveloped in silence, almost as if the Evangelists wanted to protect the privacy of this extraordinary woman. One might say that Mary comes from silence just as someone is from a certain country. How do you imagine, Pope Francis, the seasons of Mary's life, from her birth until she was assumed into heaven?

From her birth until the Annunciation, at the moment of the encounter with the angel of God, I imagine her as a normal young woman from a little village. She was brought up in a simple, ordinary way. She was open to getting married, to having a family. One thing I imagine is that she loved the Holy Scriptures: she knew the Word of God, she had received teaching from her family, from the heart. Then, after the conception of Jesus she was still a normal woman: Mary is normality, she is a woman whom any woman in this world can say she is able to imitate. No strange things in her life, a normal woman: even in her virginal marriage, chaste in that setting of virginity, she worked, went shopping, helped her Son, and helped her husband.

There is a magnificent verse in one of the Psalms: "You are the most handsome of men" (45:3). I like to think that the most handsome of men went looking for the most beautiful of all women. That is the great reality of Mary's Immaculate Conception. Sometimes it even frightens me, all this beauty hidden in one history. But I am struck by the style: Mary tiptoes into history, and she tiptoes out of it. This is also the style of her Son. But what does it mean, in concrete terms, that Mary was born without original sin?

It means that she was born, as I like to say, even *before* Eve. This is not true from the chronological point of view, but I like to think that she was born before the moment in which Eve was deceived, seduced.

Because Mary was not the victim of deceit, she did not undergo the consequences of it. But she was also born afterward because in the vision of the Church re-creation is more important than creation. Creation begins with Adam and then Eve, and both of them were created in the image and likeness of God. Re-creation begins from Mary, from a single woman. We could think of the single women who keep the house going, who bring up children on their own. And look, Mary is even more alone than that. Alone she begins this history, which continues with Joseph and the family; but in the beginning, re-creation is the dialogue between God and a single woman.

This juncture is fundamental: Christian history begins with a woman who is capable of being amazed. A poet said that one who loses the capacity for being amazed ages prematurely. It could almost be said that if we cannot be surprised—or allow God to surprise us—we don't know what we are missing in life.

That's exactly right, because God is the God of surprises. Amazement is a human virtue that is no longer found on the market. Take a child, show him something that grabs his attention: he is amazed right away, amazement is the virtue of children. If we lose the capacity to be amazed, we cannot understand Mary. To understand Mary we must go back, become children, feel the amazement of children, say "Hail, Mary" like a child, with the heart of a child, with the eyes of the heart, which our culture has lost. We need to rediscover amazement in the life of the Church. We need to marvel.

The Beauty of a Woman
in Whom God Dwells

[Every December 8] we contemplate the beauty of Mary Immaculate. The Gospel, which tells the story of the Annunciation, helps us to understand what we are celebrating, above all through the greeting of the angel. Gabriel addresses Mary with a word that is not easy to translate, that means "lavished with grace," "created by grace," "full of grace" (cf. Lk 1:28). Before calling her Mary, he calls her *full of grace,* and thus reveals the new name that God has given her and that suits her better than the name given to her by her parents. We too call her this, in every *Hail Mary.*

What does *full of grace* mean? That Mary is full of the presence of God. And if God dwells in her completely, there is no room for sin in her. This is an extraordinary thing, because unfortunately everything in the world is contaminated with evil. Every one of us can look within and see a dark side. Even the greatest saints were sinners, and all realities, even the most beautiful, are tainted by evil: all of them, except for Mary. She is the only "oasis ever green" of humanity, the only one uncontaminated, created immaculate in order to welcome fully with her "yes" the God who was coming into the world, and in this way to begin a new history.

Every time we acknowledge her as *full of grace,* we give her the greatest compliment, the same one that God gave to her. One nice compliment to give to a lady is to tell her politely that she looks young for her age. When we call Mary *full of grace,* in a certain sense we are also saying this to her, at the highest level. In fact we acknowledge her as forever young, because she was never aged by sin. There is only one thing that truly ages us, ages us on the inside: not time, but sin. Sin makes us old because it *hardens the heart.* It closes it, makes it sluggish, makes it wither. But the one *full of grace* is empty of sin. So she is forever young, she is "younger than sin," she is "the youngest of the human race," to quote *The Diary of a Country Priest* by Georges Bernanos.

Today the Church compliments Mary by calling

her "all beautiful," *tota pulchra*. Just as her youth is not a matter of years, so also her beauty does not consist in the external. Mary, as the Gospel shows, is not extraordinary in appearance: from an ordinary family, she lived humbly in Nazareth, a village almost no one had ever heard of. And she was not famous: even when the angel visited her, no one knew about it; there was no reporter there that day. Nor did Our Lady live a life of ease, but of concerns and fears: she was "greatly troubled" (Lk 1:29), the Gospel says, and when the angel "departed from her" (v. 38) there were even more problems.

Nonetheless, the one *full of grace* lived *a beautiful life*. What was her secret? We can grasp it by taking another look at the scene of the Annunciation. In many paintings Mary is depicted sitting in front of the angel with a little book in her hand. This book is the Scripture. So Mary was accustomed to listening to God and spending time with him. The Word of God was her secret: close to her heart, he then took flesh in her womb. By staying with God, dialoguing with him in every circumstance, Mary made her life beautiful. It is not the appearance, not that which passes, but the heart set on God that makes life beautiful. Today let us look with joy to the one who is *full of grace*. Let us ask her to help us to remain young, saying *"no" to sin,* and to live a beautiful life, saying *"yes" to God.*

Hail, Mary, full of grace,

the Lord is with you.

Blessed are you among women

and blessed is the fruit of your womb, Jesus.

Holy Mary, Mother of God,

pray for us sinners,

now and at the hour of our death.

Amen.

The Lord Is with You

In the second verse of the Hail Mary, *we say "the Lord is with you." I think that for Mary, God is not an intellectual concept. God is a search, and like every search it is troubled, even dangerous. When we say, "the Lord is with you," it is like saying: "Take a look, in your heart there is a love story with God under way." And yet in all love stories, along with love and surprise there also comes fear. Can we become afraid when God knocks on the door and calls us to an adventure?*

Of course, and this is a good sign. If a young man of today, a young woman of today, hears a special call from the Lord and is not afraid, that means something is missing. However, when along with enthusiasm for that call there is also the experience of fear, then we can move forward, because God calls us to great things, and if we are sincere we know our lowliness. It is normal. It is human to be afraid of making mistakes. It is human to be afraid that a calling is a fantasy or an illusion, especially for young people who feel the vocation to follow Jesus more closely in consecrated life, or those called to the priesthood, or those called to marriage, comme il faut. There is an open fear and a closed fear. Closed fear is that which makes you a slave: you are a child of fear. That is useless, it doesn't allow you to grow. Open fear is the holy awe of God. I am afraid, I am fearful, but I go forward feeling fear and assurance at the same time.

When we find ourselves facing a decision, we often find someone who says to us: "Don't be afraid; I am close to you, I am with you." But at the crucial moment of decision, man finds himself tremendously alone. That day, in that room, Mary was alone with her God. I confess, Pope Francis, that when I sometimes think of Mary, what comes to mind is the figure of the pope, when he must make a decision before God and before the Church. I think that he is the most solitary of all the solitaries in the world, and I would like to ask you: how does one keep from crumbling under the weight of such fear?

Not only the pope: many men and women, at difficult times in their lives, must make a decision. A good decision is made with the help of advice, with consultations, but at the decisive moment you are alone with the Lord. Mary is alone at that moment: she is frightened, at first she doesn't really understand, because she had never imagined a call like that, she expresses her difficulties. But when she receives the explanations, then she goes forward: alone, but with the Lord. We see in Mary the courage of a young woman who, after understanding what is expected from her, agrees to continue.

Mary's first words in the Gospels are a question: how is this possible? Saying to a person "the Lord is with you" is making a proclamation. Pope Francis, thinking back to your call to the priesthood in Argentina, did you sense the appeal of this voice? God's call is for setting people free, from fear as well. The dream of dictatorship, instead, is to make them slaves. One day I met a mom, one of the moms of the Plaza de Mayo, who told me about her daughter who had been thrown out of an airplane during the death flights. How does one find the courage to say to a mom who has been told that her son or daughter has died, "the Lord is with you"?

To a mom who has suffered what the moms of the Plaza de Mayo have suffered, I allow everything. She can say anything she wants because it is impossible to understand the sorrow of a mom. One of them said to me: "I would like to see at least the body, the bones of my daughter, to know where she was buried." It is a terrible experience, that of a woman who has had a child torn from her. There is a kind of memory that I call "maternal memory," something physical, a memory of flesh and bone. This memory can explain the anguish too. Many times they say: "But where was the Church in that moment, why didn't it defend us?" I keep quiet, and try to just be there for them. The desperation of the moms of the Plaza de Mayo is terrible. All we can do is be there for them and respect their grief, hold their hands, but it is difficult.

If we read the Gospel through the eyes of Mary, one thing appears crystal-clear: wherever Mary is, there is an extraordinary concentration of the Holy Spirit. But Mary was a woman like any other: she did not understand right away how the story would end. She too had to slowly come to grips with a mystery that was unraveled bit by bit. An author you like a great deal, Romano Guardini, writes that Mary's is a "faith that perseveres in the incomprehensible, waiting for light from God." Mary had to discover the Mystery a little at a time: training her thinking, declaring herself as one of God's poor, admitting that what is impossible for men is possible for God. She trusted.

She trusted. At the moment of the presentation of Jesus in the Temple, the elderly Simeon says something to Mary, a caution: "Behold, he is here for the fall and rise of many in Israel, and as a sign of contradiction—and a sword will pierce your heart also" (Lk 2:34–35). Then, twelve years later, when Jesus stayed in Jerusalem, Mary felt that terrible anguish: here is the moment of the sword, she must have thought, just like Simeon had prophesied to her. This is why she followed her Son. Alone at the moment of the Annunciation and alone at the moment of her Son's death.

Faith: Fidelity and Trust

Today we look at one of the Lord's wonders: Mary! A creature humble and weak like us, chosen to be Mother of God. Mother of her Creator.

Looking precisely to Mary, I would like to reflect with you on three realities: first, *God surprises us;* second, *God asks us for faithfulness;* third, *God is our strength.*

God surprises us; it is precisely in poverty, in weakness, in humility that he manifests himself to us and gives us his love that saves us, heals us, brings us strength. He asks only that we follow his Word and trust in him.

This is the experience of the Virgin Mary: confronted with the angel's proclamation, she does not hide her wonder. It is the amazement of seeing that God, to become man, has chosen none other than her, an ordinary young woman from Nazareth, who does not live in palaces of power and wealth, has not achieved extraordinary feats, but is open to God, knows how to trust him, even if she does not understand everything: she replies, "Behold, I am the handmaid of the Lord. May it be done to me according to your word" (Lk 1:38). God always surprises us, ruins our plans, makes a mess of our projects, and says to us: trust me, do not be afraid, let yourself be surprised, get out of yourself and follow me!

Today let us all think about whether we are afraid of what God may be asking or is asking of us. Do I allow myself to be surprised by God, as Mary did, or do I close myself up in my certainties, material certainties, intellectual certainties, ideological certainties, the certainties of my plans? Do I truly let God enter into my life? How do I respond to him?

The second point: to remember Christ always, the remembrance of Jesus Christ, and this is to persevere in faith; *God* surprises us with his love, but *asks for faithfulness in following him*. We can become "unfaithful," but he cannot, he is "the faithful one" and asks the same faithfulness from us. Let us think about how many times we have become excited about something, some initiative, some effort, but then in the face of the first problems have thrown in the towel. And this, unfortunately, also happens in fundamental decisions, like that of marriage. The difficulty of being constant, of being faithful to the decisions made, to the commitments entered. Often it is easy to say "yes," but then we fail to repeat this "yes" every day. We fail to be faithful.

Mary said her "yes" to God, a "yes" that disrupted her humble life in Nazareth, but it was not the only one; on the contrary, it was only the first "yes" of many spoken within her heart in her moments of joy as well as those of sorrow, a repeated "yes" that was crowned with the one she gave beneath the cross. All you moms, think about how far Mary's faithfulness to God went: to see her only Son on the cross. The faithful woman, still standing, destroyed on the inside, but faithful and strong.

And I wonder: am I an "on-again, off-again" Christian, or am I a Christian always? The culture that sees things as disposable and relative also enters into the life of faith. God asks us to be faithful to him every day, in our routine activities, and adds that even if at times we are not faithful to him, he is always faithful and in his mercy does not grow weary of reaching out to pick us up again, of encouraging us to get back on the path, to return to him and tell him about our weakness so that he may give us his strength. And this is the definitive path: always with the Lord, even in our weaknesses, even in our sins. Never go the way of just-for-now. That kills us. Faith is definitive fidelity, like that of Mary.

The last point: *God is our strength.* After the Annunciation, the first thing Mary does is an act of charity for her elderly relative Elizabeth; and the first words she speaks are "My soul magnifies the Lord," a song of praise and thanksgiving to God not only for what he has done in her but for his action in all of salvation history. Everything is his gift. If we can understand that everything is a gift from God, what happiness in our hearts! Everything is his gift. He is our strength! Saying "thank you" is so easy, and yet so hard! How often do we say "thank you" in our family? It is one of the key words in getting along together. "Excuse me," "sorry," "thank you": using these three words, the family moves forward. How often do we say "thank you" in our family? How often do we say "thank you" to those who help us, are close to us, are there for us in our lives? So often we take everything for granted! And this also happens with God. It is easy to go to the Lord to ask for something, but to go to thank him that is an inconvenience: "Oh, I don't feel like it."

Continuing the Eucharist, let us plead for Mary's intercession, that she may help us to let God surprise us without resistance, to be faithful to him every day, to praise him and thank him because he is our strength.

Hail, Mary, full of grace,

the Lord is with you.

Blessed are you among women

and blessed is the fruit of your womb, Jesus.

Holy Mary, Mother of God,

pray for us sinners,

now and at the hour of our death.

Amen

Blessed Are You
Among Women

First the angel and then her cousin Elizabeth say something amazing to Mary: "Blessed are you among women." I connect the verb "bless" with the concept of hope: there is something that can come forth from beyond the difficulties. In simple terms, what does it mean that Mary among all women was the one who was blessed?

Mary is blessed because she was born faultless. She is without sin. She was chosen to be the Mother, to give flesh to God, and isn't giving flesh to God a blessing? When our moms conceived and then gave birth to us, weren't they blessed and happy because they had given life to a child? So let's think about Mary, who conceives by none other than God and gives flesh to God: a blessing much greater than that of our moms.

If we read the Gospel, we understand that Mary's living room was the street. Mary lived an ordinary life, the kind we were told about by Fr. Tonino Bello, that she went to the market and haggled. I see the same anguish there. Letting Mary onto the street does not mean trivializing her, but taking into account the context where she got her training, with a simple life, to be available for God and his call.

Mary is a woman who lived a normal life.

What is normality?

Living among the people and like the people. It is abnormal to live without roots in a people, without a connection with a historical people. In those conditions there comes a sin that is very much to the liking of Satan, our enemy: the sin of the *elite*. The *elite* does not know what it means to live among the people, and when I talk about the *elite* I do not mean a social class: I am talking about an attitude of the soul. One can belong to a Church of *elites*. But as the [Second Vatican] Council says in *Lumen Gentium*, the Church is the holy faithful people of God (cf. *LG* 12). The Church is a people, the people of God. And the devil likes the *elites*.

Maybe this is why the normality of Mary is so striking for us. The theme of blessing recalls that of affection: the Christian God is an affectionate God. In the apostolic exhortation Evangelii Gaudium, *you wrote, "Whenever we look to Mary, we come to believe once again in the revolutionary nature of love and tenderness" (EG 288). If you, thinking of Mary, evoke these two words, someone probably gave rise to them within your heart. Who presented this tenderness of Mary to you when you were a child?*

Some of the women of my family (my mom and grandmas, one of them in particular) and the nun who prepared me for first communion, silent, good. I remember her as the teacher of love for Our Lady. A very profound experience is connected to this woman. On October 17, 1986, I returned to Argentina from Germany, and they told me she had died that very day. The next day I sat down beside the coffin early in the morning, and until three in the afternoon I did not move from that pew in church, praying and remembering. Then I accompanied her to the cemetery. Maybe this sister is the very woman who taught me the most about Mary. Her name was Dolores.

You often recall one of your grandmas . . .

A grandma of mine with whom I had a special bond. My grandparents on my father's side lived less than a block from our house, and when my mom had her second child, thirteen months after me, my grandma came every morning to get me and brought me back home around four in the afternoon. I could say that my mother tongue is Piedmontese [a dialect in the region where Pope Francis's family lived], because my grandparents spoke with each other in this dialect and this had a big influence on my life.

The Smile of Feeling Like Part of the People

Beginning the year by commemorating God's goodness in the motherly face of Mary, in the motherly face of the Church, in the faces of our own mothers protects us from the corrosive illness of "spiritual orphanhood," that orphanhood which the soul experiences when it feels that it has no mother and lacks the tenderness of God. That orphanhood which we experience when we are deprived of any sense of belonging to a family, to a people, to a land, to our God. That orphanhood which finds a place in the narcissistic heart that knows only how to look at itself and its own interests, and which grows when we forget that life was a gift, that we have received it from others, and that we are called to share it in this common home.

This self-absorbed orphanhood is what led Cain to say, "Am I my brother's keeper?" (Gen 4:9), as if to say: he does not belong to me, I do not acknowledge him. Such an attitude of spiritual orphanhood is a cancer that silently consumes and degrades the soul. So little by little we degrade ourselves, since nobody belongs to us and we belong to nobody; I degrade the earth because it does not belong to me, I degrade others because they do not belong to me, I degrade God because I do not belong to him . . . And we end up degrading ourselves, because we forget who we are, the divine "name" that we have.

The loss of the ties that bind us, typical of our fragmented and divided culture, leads to the growth of this sense of orphanhood, and therefore of great emptiness and loneliness. The lack of physical (and not virtual) contact is numbing our hearts (cf. encyclical letter *Laudato Si'* 49), making them lose their capacity for tenderness and wonder, for pity and compassion. Spiritual orphanhood makes us lose the memory of what it means to be children, to be grandchildren, to be parents, to be grandparents, to be friends, to be believers. It makes us lose the memory of the value of play, of singing, of laughter, of rest, of spontaneity.

Celebrating the feast of the Holy Mother of God brings back to our faces the smile of feeling like part of the people, of feeling that we belong, of knowing that it is only within a community, a family, that persons can find the "climate," the "warmth" that allows us to learn to grow as human beings and not as mere objects meant to "consume and be consumed." Celebrating the feast of the Holy Mother of God reminds us that we are not bargaining chips or input devices. We are children. We are family. We are the people of God.

Celebrating the Holy Mother of God impels us to create and care for common spaces that can give us a sense of belonging, of rootedness, that can make us feel at home in our cities, in communities that unite and support us (cf. *LS* 151).

Jesus Christ, at the moment of the greatest gift of his life on the cross, did not want to keep anything for himself, and in giving his life also gave us his Mother. He said to Mary: Behold your son, behold your children. And we want to welcome her into our homes, into our families, into our communities, into our countries. We want to look into her motherly eyes. Into that gaze which sets us free from orphan-hood; that gaze which reminds us that we are broth-ers: that I belong to you, that you belong to me, that we are of the same flesh. That gaze which teaches us that we must learn to take care of life in the same way and with the same tenderness with which she took care of it: sowing hope, sowing the sense of belong-ing, sowing brotherhood.

Hail, Mary, full of grace,

the Lord is with you.

Blessed are you among women

and blessed is the fruit of your womb, Jesus.

Holy Mary, Mother of God,

pray for us sinners,

now and at the hour of our death.

Amen.

And Blessed Is the Fruit of Your Womb, Jesus

I always think that the verb "bless" is strictly connected to the verb "curse." A curse can be removed with a blessing. The sin of Eve brings painful consequences with it (cf. Gen 3:16), while to Mary, God says through the angel: "Rejoice, full of grace" (cf. Lk 1:28), and her cousin Elizabeth, "filled with the holy Spirit," exults: "blessed is the fruit of your womb" (Lk 1:41–42). It almost seems that Mary is the answer to Satan's gibes. Pope Francis, the theme of the devil is crucial in your magisterium: why does this unclean being hate Mary so much?

Because Mary bore the Savior in her womb. She brought regeneration to the world. She brought God among men. She was the one who climbed the stairs so that God could come to us. Fr. [Marko Ivan] Rupnik created an image of the Madonna with Child. The hands of Our Lady are the stairs on which Jesus descends, as he holds the scroll of the Law in one hand and grasps Mary's mantle in the other. God grasped onto a woman in order to come to us. This is a very evocative image of that self-abasement of God, who made himself utterly close to us precisely through a woman, through the willing "yes" of one of us. This is why Satan hates Our Lady so much: because she was the instrument of God's self-abasement.

And above all she is the one who unmasks all the lies that Satan tells about Jesus. The verse that closes the first part of the Hail Mary *introduces none other than the Son: "and blessed is the fruit of your womb, Jesus." One time I read an essay by a third grader. Talking about his mom, he wrote: "If you have given me life, it means that for one day you were God. You're great, mom!" I, as a child, think of a child as a blessing. But going around the world we discover that for many women a son or a daughter can also be a curse. There are women who—with abortion, with abandonment— do not accept a child. But can a child really be a curse?*

A child is never a curse. He may be a cross for his mom. The cause of beatification was recently opened for a young woman from Rome who died in her twenties. Struck with an illness while she was pregnant, she refused treatment in order to protect her child until he was born. For her, that child was truly a blessing. There is a word that is very dear to me: *tenderness*. The other day a gentleman told me, speaking of humanity, that we have lost the capacity to love, we have lost the memory of caresses, the memory of tenderness. Today we need the revolution of tenderness. Let's think of the image of the Mother of God: it is the image of tenderness that protects, her cheek against the cheek of her Son. What we need is Our Lady of Tenderness: this is the blessing. Without tenderness one cannot understand a mom, without tenderness one cannot understand Mary. In the cathedral of Bari I contemplated the icon of the Virgin Hodegetria: this was the first time I had seen the Child half-naked and covered by Mary with her mantle. Mary covers our nakedness; a mom is the only one who can understand a child, because she knows him naked from her belly, from her womb, she gives birth to a naked child. Then Mary receives Christ naked at the foot of the cross, and covers him again. Mary is a blessing for us because she is the mother of our nakedness: evil and sin strip us bare, but she always covers us up again.

I always think that Mary could have said "no." Too many people may think that Mary was forced to say "yes"; instead, she could have answered "no," and this is why her "yes" was even greater. We live in a world that dreams of being free by making others slaves; Mary affirms that in order to be free, one must be a servant of the Lord. As Saint Augustine maintained, to serve is to reign. Mary's freedom is a sign of contradiction.

There is a moment of waiting between the angel's proposal and Mary's response. In a beautiful passage, Saint Bernard directly addresses Our Lady and implores her: "Hurry up, hurry up, we need salvation!" (cf. *Homilies* 4, 8–9).

And where did Mary find the strength to bear the weight of this call?

Mary was not omnipotent, she was a normal woman: full of grace, but normal. The power is that grace of the Holy Spirit. Mary is full of the Holy Spirit, who accompanies her for her entire life.

When I also think about my personal history, I am always amazed that there is a God who decides to depend on the freedom of men. And yet he is a God who sometimes causes fear: history is full of calls from God that have not received any answer from men. Why is God so reckless when it comes to dialoguing with humanity?

Because he is dialoguing with his children. Let's think of the father of the prodigal son (cf. Lk 15:11–32): he dialogues with both sons, the one who went away to lead a dissolute life and the other, the perfect one, who, however, reveals the ambition to climb into his dad's place. Both of them, in other words, are far from the father's love. God takes a risk with us like that father who was waiting every day for the return of the younger and, the Gospel says, sees him coming from afar. When the father realizes that the older son is not participating in the celebration, he goes out to call him. That father bet on his sons. The mystics talk about divine madness, and the love of God for his people is a kind of madness: I have not chosen you because you are the most intelligent, the greatest, the strongest; you are the smallest in the world (cf. Dt 7:7). That is how God loves.

Pope John Paul I said that God, in addition to being Father, is also a mom. On this journey through the Hail Mary *I have met a philosopher who opened up for me a beautiful perspective on motherhood. According to writer Luisa Muraro, "There are no mothers; there are ordinary women who become mothers, made such by a need, by a cry, in responding to which they remember and then immediately forget their own needs." It is beautiful to put the other ahead of oneself.*

Very poetic and true. But in saying that God is dad and mom, Pope John Paul I didn't say anything strange. God has said it about himself, through Isaiah and other prophets: he has presented himself as a mom: "I protect you like a mom, a mom cannot forget her child, and even if she should do so I never could" (cf. Is 49:15).

Pope Francis, when you read this passage does it remind you of your mom?

Yes, we owe our lives to a woman. And when we say the *Hail Mary* we establish a natural connection between Our Lady and our moms.

The Maternal Tenderness of God

Far from wanting to understand or dominate the situation, Mary is the woman who knows how to preserve, meaning protect, *safeguard* in her heart God's movement in the life of his people. Through her womb she learned to listen to the heartbeat of her Son, and this taught her, for the rest of her life, to discover the cadences of God in history. She learned to be a mother, and in that apprenticeship gave Jesus the beautiful experience of knowing himself to be Son. In Mary, the eternal Word not only became flesh but learned to recognize the maternal tenderness of God. With Mary, the God-Child learned to listen to the yearnings, the anguish, the joys and hopes of the people of the promise. With her he discovered himself as Son of the holy faithful people of God.

In the Gospels, Mary appears as a woman of few words, without big speeches or showing off, but with an attentive gaze that is able to protect the life and mission of her Son, and therefore of all that he loves. She was able to safeguard the first flickers of the early Christian community, and in this way she learned to be the mother of a multitude. She drew near to the most diverse situations in order to sow hope. She accompanied the crosses carried in the silence of her children's hearts. So many devotions, so many shrines and chapels in the most isolated places, so many images throughout our homes remind us of this great truth.

Mary has given us motherly warmth, the kind that envelops us in the midst of difficulties; the motherly warmth that allows nothing and no one to extinguish in the Church's bosom the revolution of tenderness that her Son inaugurated. Wherever a mother is, there is tenderness. And Mary shows us with her motherhood that humility and tenderness are not virtues of the weak, but of the strong; she teaches us that there is no need to mistreat others in order to feel important (cf. apostolic exhortation *Evangelii Gaudium* 288). And the holy faithful people of God have always recognized and hailed her as the Holy Mother of God.

Celebrating Mary's maternity as Mother of God and our mother at the beginning of a new year means remembering one certainty that will accompany our days: we are a people with a Mother, we are not orphans.

Mothers are the most powerful antidote against our individualistic and selfish tendencies, against our isolation and indifference. A society without mothers would be not only a cold society but a society that has lost its heart, that has lost the "family feel." A society without mothers would be a society without pity, one that has left room only for calculation and speculation. Because mothers, even at the worst of times, know how to bear witness to tenderness, unconditional dedication, the power of hope. I have learned a lot from those mothers who, having children in prison or laid up in hospital beds or shackled by the slavery of drugs, come rain or shine, come what may, they do not give up and keep fighting to give their children the best they can. Or those mothers who, in the refugee camps or even in the midst of war, are able to embrace and bear without wavering the sufferings of their children. Mothers who literally give their lives so that none of their children may be lost. Wherever a mother is there is unity, there is belonging, the belonging of children.

Hail, Mary, full of grace,

the Lord is with you.

Blessed are you among women

and blessed is the fruit of your womb, Jesus.

Holy Mary, Mother of God,

pray for us sinners,

now and at the hour of our death.

Amen.

Holy Mary

"Holy Mary" begins the second part of the Hail Mary. *It contains the words of the angel and of Elizabeth, which come from the Gospel of Luke. It is beautiful that the second part of this prayer begins with the theme of holiness, a theme that for you, Pope Francis, is very close to your heart. In the apostolic exhortation* Gaudete et Exsultate, *you wrote: "I like to contemplate the holiness present in the patience of God's people . . . a holiness found in our next-door neighbors, those who, living in our midst, reflect God's presence." And you add a wonderful image: "the middle class of holiness." In what does Mary's holiness consist? And what do you mean by this middle class of holiness?*

Mary's holiness is easily told: perhaps not so easy to understand, but easily told. It is the fullness of the Holy Spirit in her. Mary is what she is because she is filled with Spirit. The expression "the middle class of holiness" is not my own: I stole it from a French writer, Joseph Malègue. He is the one who dared to say: "The scandal and the difficulty is not understanding if God exists, but it is understanding that God became Christ." This is the scandal. And Our Lady is at the center of this scandal. Holiness is at the center of this scandal. We cannot understand holiness without understanding that God became Jesus Christ, meaning true man like us and true God. Mary's holiness is the fullness of the Holy Spirit, and our holiness is allowing God to become Christ in us, in the little things of every day. I wanted to cite in the apostolic exhortation on holiness, *Gaudete et Exsultate,* a little example that I like a lot. A lady meets a friend at the market; they start talking and slowly slip into gossip. But this woman makes herself a promise not to speak evil of anyone. She stops in time, succeeds in not destroying the good name of others. Here is another little step toward holiness, the holiness of the everyday, of simplicity, of the middle class, as Malègue would say.

I am fascinated by the words used in your magisterium in recent years: not to surprise God, but rather to allow God to surprise us; not to encounter God, but to allow God to encounter us. Correct me if I am wrong: perhaps holiness is not doing things for God, but allowing God to do things for me. More than filling oneself, it means emptying oneself: allowing God to come through. In reality I find it hard to believe that God would be so stubborn as to love someone like me. I feel ashamed of his inclination toward me. It is as if he were saying: "You are a sinner, and I have to save you as soon as possible." I have a hard time accepting the idea that God, as if in plain clothes, behind the people around me, is doing something for me, because that makes me feel weak, deficient . . .

That's just it: it is allowing God to work in us, through others. Holiness is letting God do it. We must not forget that one of the enemies of holiness is the Pelagian spirit, meaning the insistence on the human will and not on grace: "I want to do it myself, I'll do it, I . . ." It is God who does everything, God is always "first." In the book of the prophet Jeremiah, in fact, the Lord talks about his action on behalf of the people using the image of the almond branch (cf. Jer 1:11–12). Why? Because it is the first to blossom. It is spring. The Lord is always ahead of us, his action is always ahead of us. I am reminded of a poetic way of describing God, through a dialogue between an oak and an almond tree. The oak asked the almond tree: "Tell me about God." And the almond tree blossomed.

The answer is to blossom! It is an answer connected to beauty: the beauty of a painting, of a gaze, of a meeting. How much does beauty matter in encountering Christ, Pope Francis?

It is important. The angel does not say to Mary: "You are full of intellect, you are intelligent, you are full of virtue, you are an ultragood woman." No: "You are full of grace," meaning of that which is unmerited, of beauty. Our Lady is the one who is beautiful par excellence. Beauty is one of the human dimensions that too often we overlook. We talk about truth, about goodness, and we leave beauty out. And yet it is just as important as the others. It is important to find God in beauty.

It is wonderful to be seekers of beauty. It occurs to me that every time I see my mom doing the laundry, while she is washing my dirty clothes, I think that if one day my mom becomes a saint it will be because she did the laundry with a smile. And I am also reminded of the verses of a female Bulgarian poet [Blaga Dimitrova] whom I connect immediately with the theme of holiness: "No fear that they may tread on me. Downtrodden, the grass becomes a path." Beauty is Mary, who shows us how to let ourselves be trodden upon, perhaps even made fun of by people who consider themselves intelligent . . .

Mary is trodden upon, yes.

Let's think of the madonnari: the people walk on their images of Our Lady, and they continue to paint.

Mary was trodden upon, denigrated even during her lifetime. Think of the comments on Calvary: "Look at the criminal's mom, how she must have raised him . . ."

Downtrodden like the moms of inmates outside of the prisons, according to that terrible image you use in speaking of the Church.

Many times while riding the bus I passed the prison of Villa Devoto in Buenos Aires. There were all the moms lined up and everyone saw them, these women in line to get in, to visit a son. It is not hard to imagine the humiliations a woman must suffer, the pat downs. But it doesn't matter, it's for a son. They let themselves be trodden upon, what matters is the son. To Mary what was important was her Son. Not the comments of others. That was why she was on Calvary. But there even her Son abandons her, not only because he abandons life. He says to her, "Now you will have others," and gives us all a mom, who gives birth to us on the cross.

Act of Veneration of the Immaculate in Piazza di Spagna

Virgin holy and immaculate,
the honor of our people and the caring protector
of our city,
we come to you with confidence and love.

You are All-beautiful, O Mary!
There is no sin in you.

Stir up in all of us a renewed desire for holiness:
may our words shine with the splendor of truth,
may our works resound with the song of charity,
may purity and chastity dwell in our bodies and
hearts,
may all the beauty of the Gospel become
present in our lives.

You are All-beautiful, O Mary!
The Word of God became flesh in you.

Help us to keep listening attentively to the voice
of the Lord:
may the cry of the poor never leave us
indifferent,
may the suffering of the sick and needy not find
us distracted,
may the solitude of the elderly and the frailty of
children touch our hearts,
may every human life be always loved and
venerated by us all.

You are All-beautiful, O Mary!
In you is the fullness of joy in the blessed life
with God.

Grant that we may not forget the meaning of
our earthly journey:
may the gentle light of faith illuminate our days,
may the consoling power of hope guide our
steps,
may the contagious warmth of love enliven our
hearts,
may all our eyes look steadily there, to God,
where true joy is.

You are All-beautiful, O Mary!
Hear our prayer, attend to our plea:
may the beauty of God's merciful love in Jesus
    be within us,
may it be this divine beauty that saves us, our
    city, the whole world.

Amen.

Hail, Mary, full of grace,

the Lord is with you.

Blessed are you among women

and blessed is the fruit of your womb, Jesus.

Holy Mary, *Mother of God,*

pray for us sinners,

now and at the hour of our death.

Amen.

Mother of God

"Holy Mary, Mother of God": perhaps we do not think enough about the fact that in the Hail Mary *we do not say "Mother of Jesus" but "Mother of God." The memory goes back to that famous Council of Ephesus in 431: two hundred bishops in front of a people who were acclaiming Mary as "Mother of God," in Greek* Theotókos. *It is beautiful to think that God, the God they always taught us to imagine as elderly, with a white beard, is a child in the arms of a mother. There is no longer any distance between me and God.*

Those people knew what they were saying. They were not only shouting; according to tradition, they were holding clubs. That was what the bishops would have expected if they did not proclaim Our Lady "Mother of God": a club . . .

There's a world of difference between saying "Mother of Jesus" and saying "Mother of God."

The people knew the truth. Mary is truly Mother of God. God makes himself smaller. This makes it possible to understand what Paul, in the letter to the Philippians, said about the Son of God, who, "though he was in the form of God . . . humbled himself, becoming obedient to death, even death on a cross" (Phil 2:6–8). God took on all of our sins. Paul was thinking: God became sin. He did not commit sins, but he made himself sin for us, and Mary is the mom of the Holy One and of the sinners, of us all.

There is an incredible symbiosis between Mother and Son: in Bethlehem, in Egypt, in Jerusalem we always find them together, the Mother with the Son. I like what Saint Louis-Marie Grignion de Montfort said: "It is easier to divide the light from the sun than it is to separate Mary from Jesus." Perhaps Mary too experienced a dark night in her faith, above all in those thirty years of hidden life: they had said to her, "He will be great, he will be son of God!" and she saw Jesus doing the things that all the other children were doing, and then fixing chairs, tables, windows . . . For Mary as well, faith must have been a fight. Who knows how many thoughts, how much obscurity was even within her heart, thinking: "This is my son, but he is also my God."

That is the astonishment of Mary. And then the last fight, because on the cross there was not only the torment of Jesus, but also Mary's fight. Let's take the *Stabat Mater* by Jacopone da Todi. The *Stabat Mater* has captivated many composers, it has attracted them because it is a mystery: the mystery of Mary at the foot of the cross. In this struggle, she struggled too: like Jesus, the night before, struggled in the Garden of Gethsemane in accepting the will of the Father.

Was Mary troubled?

She was troubled. One cannot conceive of holiness without disquiet.

A hardship that, in the life of Mary, must also be closely associated with the figure of Joseph, although he is not mentioned in the Hail Mary. *There is an image in one of the litanies that I always repeat to myself: "Holy Mary, spouse of Joseph." Teresa of Avila dedicated her first convent to Saint Joseph. One of the most beautiful legends that you, Pope Francis, keep telling to the world is that of Saint Joseph asleep. Who was Joseph in Mary's life?*

He was the husband. And Mary certainly never said to Joseph: "I am God's mom, you are God's employee." Instead, she said: "You are my husband, I am a virgin" (Joseph is too) "but you are my husband." She was subordinate to her husband, as the culture of her time would have it. She prepared his meals, talked with him, together spoke about the Son, they shared the anguish when the Child, at the age of twelve, remained behind in Jerusalem, the anguish of a husband and wife, the anguish of parents. Normality in virginity. And she listened to Joseph. Joseph made the big decisions, which was normal for the time. Joseph received messages from God in his dreams. She is the one full of grace, he is the just man, the man observant of the Word of God. A beautiful couple.

There was also an annunciation to Joseph. The angel appears to him in a dream and urges him not to be afraid, because salvation history had a role for him as well.

Yes, the annunciation to Joseph. And let's not forget the delicacy with which Joseph thinks of repudiating Mary secretly, to avoid hurting her. He makes all the preparations for his departure, even though the people may have said: "But what a terrible person, he has abandoned a pregnant young woman." He was about to take the blame upon himself, because he is "the just man," the man of justice. The angel proclaims the truth to him, and he obeys.

Pope Francis, I am struck by something that you do every time you are about to go on a trip: you go to the basilica of Saint Mary Major, where there is the image of Mary Salus populi romani, *"salvation of the Roman people," and leave a bouquet of flowers. The gesture of a child going to his mom. I am struck by your eyes when they meet the gaze of Mary: what does a pope see in Mary's eyes?*

It's a long story, that of Saint Mary Major. Before becoming pope, I often came to Rome for a synod or a meeting of the dicasteries of which I was a member. I would go to the churches I knew: Saint Peter's, the Gesù, Saint Ignatius, and Saint Mary Major. I often went to Saint Mary Major. I don't know why, but Our Lady, the Mother, has always drawn me. What do I think of when I look at Mary? I go back a bit to the experience with the Virgin of Guadalupe in Mexico: it is certainly wonderful to look at Our Lady, but it is even more wonderful to let Our Lady look at us, to let her look at us and to tell her everything, knowing that she is looking at us. There is an Argentine poet, a holy priest and poet, Fr. Amelio Luis Calori, very devoted to Our Lady, who died many years ago, and in allowing Our Lady to look at him he feels like a sinner and turns to poetry for help. He says he will change his ways, but finishes like this: *"Esta tarde, Señora, la promesa es sincera. Por las dudas, no olvide dejar la llave afuera"* (This evening, Lady, the promise is sincere. But just in case, don't forget to leave the key outside). Back then in Buenos Aires a mom, when she went out and there was no officer, no policeman on the corner, she would leave the key in the yard, under a rock. "Look at me, I am a sinner, but always leave the key within my reach." That poem has always done me good, and I too repeat: "Always leave the key within my reach."

The Lord Became Incarnate in Mary

Mother of God is Our Lady's most important title. But a question might arise: why do we say Mother *of God* and not Mother *of Jesus*? Some in the past wanted to stop there, but the Church has affirmed: Mary is Mother of God. We should be grateful, because these words contain a splendid truth about God and about us. Namely that ever since the Lord became incarnate in Mary, since then and forever he bears our humanity as an integral part of himself. No longer is God without man: the flesh that Jesus took from his Mother is his even now, and will be so forever. Saying Mother *of God* reminds us of this: God is close to humanity like a baby to the mother who carries him in her womb.

The word "mother" (*mater*) is also related to the word "matter." In his Mother, the God of heaven, the infinite God, became small; he became matter,

to be not only *with us* but also *like us*. Here is the miracle, here is the breakthrough: man is no longer alone, never an orphan again, he is forever a son. The year opens with this breakthrough. And we proclaim it like this, saying: "Mother of God!" It is the joy of knowing that our loneliness has been defeated. It is the beauty of knowing that we are beloved children, of knowing that this childhood of ours can never be taken away. It is to see ourselves in the mirror of the delicate infant God in his Mother's arms, and to know that humanity is dear and sacred to the Lord. Therefore serving human life is serving God, and every life, from the mother's womb to old age, in suffering and illness, when it is unsettling and even repugnant, must be welcomed, loved, and assisted.

[In the Gospel for Christmas], only one thing is said about the Mother of God: she "kept all these things, reflecting on them in her heart" (Lk 2:19). *She kept them.* She simply kept them. Mary does not speak: the Gospel does not report so much as one word from her in the whole Christmas story. In this too the Mother is united with her Son: Jesus is an infant, meaning "without speech." He, the Word of God who "in times past . . . spoke in partial and various ways" (Heb 1:1), now in the "fullness of time" (Gal 4:4) is mute. The God before whom one falls silent is a baby who cannot speak. His majesty is wordless, his mystery of love reveals itself in the small. Silent and small is the language of his kingship. The Mother follows her Son and *keeps things in silence.*

[. . .] Mary kept, the Gospel continues, "all these things, reflecting on them." What were *these things*? They were joys and sorrows: on the one hand the birth of Jesus, the love of Joseph, the visit of the shepherds, that radiant night. But on the other hand: an uncertain future; lack of shelter, "because there was no room for them in the inn" (Lk 2:7); the desolation of rejection; the disappointment of having to give birth to Jesus in a stable. Hopes and anxieties, light and shadow: *all these things* settled in the heart of Mary. And she, what did she do? She *reflected* on them, meaning that she went over them with God in her heart. She did not keep anything for herself, close anything off in solitude or smother it in bitterness; she brought everything to God. That is how she kept these things. Giving things up is how to keep them:

not allowing life to fall prey to fear, to discouragement or superstition, not closing oneself off or seeking to forget, but making everything a dialogue with
God. And God, whose heart is set on us, comes to
dwell in our lives.

Here they are, the secrets of the Mother of God:
to keep things in silence and bring them to God. This
took place, the Gospel concludes, *in her heart*. The
heart beckons us to look at the center of the person, of
the affections, of life. We too, Christians on the journey, at the beginning of the year feel the need to start
again from the center, to leave the burdens of the past
behind and start over from what matters. And here
it is in front of us today, the point of departure: the
Mother of God. Because Mary is the way God wants
us to be, the way he wants his Church to be: a tender,
humble Mother, poor in things and rich in love, free
from sin, united with Jesus, a heart for God and a life
for others. To start over, let us look to our Mother.
In her heart beats the heart of the Church. To move
forward [. . .] we must go back: start over from the
crèche, from the Mother who holds God in her arms.

Devotion to Mary is not spiritual etiquette, it

is one of the essentials of Christian life. In looking to our Mother we are encouraged to leave aside so much useless junk and rediscover what counts. The gift of the Mother, the gift of every mother and of every woman is so precious for the Church, who is mother and woman. And while the man often abstracts, affirms, and imposes ideas, the woman, the mother, knows how to keep, to connect in the heart, to give life. To prevent faith from being reduced to just ideas or doctrines, we need, all of us, a mother's heart, able to keep the tenderness of God and listen to the stirrings of man. May the Mother, God's signature of authenticity on humanity, safeguard this year and bring the peace of her Son to hearts, to our hearts, and to the world. And I invite you to greet her today like children, simply, with the greeting of the Christians of Ephesus in front of their bishops: "Holy Mother of God!" Let us say three times from the heart, all together, looking at her [turning to the statue displayed beside the altar]: "Holy Mother of God!"

Hail, Mary, full of grace,

the Lord is with you.

Blessed are you among women

and blessed is the fruit of your womb, Jesus.

Holy Mary, Mother of God,

pray for us sinners,

now and at the hour of our death.

Amen.

Pray for Us Sinners

And so we come to the verse "pray for us sinners." Salvation history, Pope Francis, begins with a question: "Adam, where are you?" (cf. Gen 3:9). Mary's story begins with an answer: "Here I am" (cf. Lk 1:38). It is as if Mom were answering for us, for all the answers we have not given. But one fact remains: paraphrasing Indro Montanelli, there are errors that smell like laundry and others that stink like a sewer. Mary is the mom of sinners, not of the corrupt. They are two completely different things.

Mary cannot be the mom of the corrupt, because the corrupt sell their moms, they sell their membership in a family, in a people. They seek only their own profit, whether this be financial, intellectual, political, of whatever kind. They make a choice that is selfish, I would call it satanic: they lock the door from the inside. And Mary cannot get in. They close themselves off, so that the only prayer for the corrupt is that an earthquake may shake them up so much that it convinces them that the world did not begin and will not end with them. This is why they close themselves off; they have no need of mother, of father, of a family, of a homeland, of belonging to a people. They cultivate nothing but selfishness, and the father of selfishness is the devil. Mary is the mother of all of us sinners, from the most to the least holy. She is Mom. I remember that my mom, speaking of us five children, used to say: "My children are like my fingers, each different from the other, but if I hurt one finger I feel the same pain that I would feel if I hurt another." Mary goes along the road with us sinners, each with his own sins. To say "Pray for us sinners" is to say: "I am a sinner, but you safeguard me." Mary is the one who safeguards us.

Sin is a lot like a knot. In your pontificate you have often referred to an image from Irenaeus of Lyon, which was also used by the [Second Vatican] Council: Mary who unties knots. Many people I meet say to me: "I am making the novena to Mary undoer of knots." It reminds me of a proverb that my mom uses every now and then as a threat: "All knots come to the comb" [All chickens come home to roost; all your sins will find you out]. And I think to myself: "It is also true that all knots come to Mary." This is a beautiful image, of the knot in a skein that Mary untangles. How much patience does this take?

The image of Irenaeus goes back to the second century. Vatican Council II uses it in *Lumen Gentium*. Irenaeus contrasts two women: the knot made by Eve, with disobedience and lack of faith, is undone by Mary, precisely with her obedience and her faith. It is an image full of meaning.

For me it is full of meaning, Pope Francis, that you insist on calling yourself a sinner on whom God continues to look with mercy. Some are amazed that a pope could call himself such a thing, but recognizing that one is a sinner is the first little step toward becoming a saint . . .

It is the reality. It is the reality. If I said I was not a sinner, I would be the most corrupt of all.

Undoing Knots

Mary's faith undoes the knot of sin (cf. *Lumen Gentium* 56). What does this mean? The council fathers [of Vatican II] borrowed an expression from Saint Irenaeus, who says: "The knot of Eve's disobedience was untied by Mary's obedience; what the virgin Eve bound through her unbelief, the Virgin Mary loosened by her faith" (*Adversus Haereses* III, 22, 4).

That's it, the "knot" of disobedience, the "knot" of disbelief. When a child disobeys Mom or Dad, we could say that a little "knot" is formed. This happens if the child is aware of what he is doing, especially if a lie is involved; in that moment he does not trust Mom and Dad. You know how often this happens! Then the relationship with the parents has to be cleansed of this flaw, and in fact there has to be an apology so that harmony and trust may be restored.

Something similar happens in our relationship with God. When we do not listen to him, do not follow his will, commit concrete actions in which we show a lack of trust in him—and this is sin—something like a knot is formed inside of us. And these knots take away our peace and serenity. They are dangerous, because several knots can become a tangle, which is even more painful and even more difficult to untie.

But for the mercy of God—we know this—nothing is impossible! Even the most intricate knots are untied with his grace. And Mary, who with her "yes" opened the door to God in order to untie the knot of ancient disobedience, is the mother who with patience and tenderness brings us to God so that he may untie the knots of our soul with his mercy as Father. Every one of us has some of these, and we can ask ourselves in our hearts: what knots are there in my life? "Father, mine cannot be undone!" But this is wrong! All knots of the heart, all knots of the conscience can be undone. Do I ask Mary that she may help me to trust in God's mercy, to undo them, to change? She, the woman of faith, will surely say to us: "Go ahead, go to the Lord: he understands you." And she leads us by the hand, Mother, Mother, to the embrace of the Father, of the Father of mercy.

Hail, Mary, full of grace,

the Lord is with you.

Blessed are you among women

and blessed is the fruit of your womb, Jesus.

Holy Mary, Mother of God,

pray for us sinners,

now and at the hour of our death.

Amen.

Now and at the Hour
of Our Death

The Hail Mary *concludes with the theme of death, which at first glance seems almost to ruin this beautiful prayer: "now and at the hour of our death." Hearing about death always brings us a bit of anguish. Pope Francis, you once said that death reminds us we are not eternal: we are men and women on a journey in time, a time that begins and a time that ends. But when death draws near, even if some call her "Sister," most of us are seized by a sense of anguish.*

The devil leads Eve to think that if she tastes the fruit she will become like a goddess, she will not undergo death. Sin is the illusion that death will never come. During a life of sin, one says he knows he will die, but he doesn't think about it. It is an illusion. And so just as the *Hail Mary* begins with the great truth of salvation, so also it ends with the great truth of the human condition, fruit of the sin that entered into the world through the envy of the devil (cf. Wis 2:24). And this is the reality. I know that it is not easy, but to think of death as the end of the journey is a reality, just as to think of Mary as full of grace is another reality. I remember one anecdote. An Argentine bishop, one of my peers, died young. They called me one morning to tell me that his death throes had begun. I went to the hospital and stayed there, and he didn't die. The doctors couldn't explain it. At a certain point a priest came who loved him as a son loves his father, and he was in effect the bishop's spiritual son. He said to us: "Wait outside." I was the last to go out, and I saw that the priest had started talking to him. After a short time he came out, we went back inside, and in five minutes the bishop was dead. A few days later I saw this priest, who is now a bishop himself, and I asked him: "What did you say to him?" "I only said to him, 'Let yourself go, have faith: it doesn't make sense staying attached to this life; let yourself go, let yourself go, let yourself go.' I gave him courage, and he went." It is beautiful: he actually got him to take on the reality of death.

When we were seminarians, they told us that in the seminaries in the past they actually practiced for a good death, they prepared for it . . .

I did that.

Really? And what did it involve?

One began to ask the Lord for mercy, but there was a whole description of the moment of death. When the sweating begins: "Merciful Jesus, have pity on us . . ." When it gets hard to breathe: "Merciful Jesus, have pity on us . . ." It was all a bit gloomy. But that was the custom at the time, it was realistic.

What did it mean, Pope Francis?

To get used to the fact that one must die. There was also a spiritual exercise: to think about one's death. To make that exercise throughout the day, to emphasize its normality. They told us that when Saint Dominic Savio was playing with his friends, they asked him: "If in this moment the Lord were to tell

you that you were about to die, what would you do?"
"Well, I would go on playing," he replied. For a saint,
death is so natural that it doesn't change the normality of life in any way.

*In the anecdote there is also that little touch of humor,
which is typical of the saints. In Jerusalem there is a
church that fascinates me, that of the Dormition of Mary.
God did not dream up death. As you recalled a little while
ago, death entered the world through the envy of the
devil. In fact, according to theology, Mary did not die.
She fell asleep, then she was assumed into heaven. She
did not experience the anguish of death. When I reflect
on this miracle, I think about what my death would be
like if Satan had not made me fall into his snare. Pope
Francis, what would you like to ask Mary for when
it comes to your death, a death that I hope is a long
way off?*

That she be near me and give me peace.

Are you able to call her "Sister," like Francis of Assisi?

That expression doesn't mean much to me. Of course, it is part of my culture, Saint Francis is brilliant, but I would not call death "Sister." I like to think of death as a final act of justice. So on the one hand death is the wages of sin, but on the other it opens the door to redemption. Living alongside of death is not part of my culture, but each one of us has his or her own culture.

One of the forms of death is, unfortunately, suicide. I always wonder, when I read stories in the newspaper about young men or young women who were not able to bear the burden of shame, of a video posted on the Internet, of a photo spread around via chat, and have decided to cut their lives short. They are deaths that are hard to stomach.

They are difficult. To some extent suicide closes the door to salvation. But I am aware that in suicides there is not complete freedom. At least I believe so. I find it helpful to think of what Saint John Mary Vianney, the Curé of Ars, said to the widow whose husband had committed suicide by jumping off a bridge: "Madam, between the bridge and the river is the mercy of God." I believe that in suicide there is not complete freedom. Nevertheless this is solely a matter of a personal opinion and not a dogmatic one.

In prison they told me that there are young prisoners who are furious because they are unable to commit suicide. They drum up the courage to act, but it almost seems that at the last moment life mounts a comeback and does not agree to go. It is the emptiness of the soul. What do you feel, Pope Francis, in the face of the sensation of loneliness and abandonment of the younger generations?

We too are guilty of that abandonment and of that loneliness, because with our culture, with what we offer we have deprived those young people of their roots. We have offered a culture without concreteness, a "fluid" culture, to use the formula of one philosopher; I would even call it "gaseous." Without roots. I think that our civilization is guilty. Young people today need to become rooted. Mary never lost her roots. She is the daughter of Israel, the daughter of Jerusalem. She was always faithful to her roots, but she went further, much further. But in life one cannot go further without holding on to the roots. Giving roots to the flower, in order to produce the tree and then the fruit.

But you have launched a synod of young people at which stories are told of youths who had the courage to face death itself for an even greater ideal. This brings hope.

Yes, and it also makes us think of the fact that Mary was sixteen, seventeen years old, no more, at the moment of the Annunciation. She is the first guest invited to the synod.

Mother of Hope

Mary is not a woman who loses heart in the face of life's uncertainties, especially when nothing seems to be going right. Nor is she a woman who protests with violence or rants against her lot in life, which often shows us a hostile face. She is instead a woman who listens: do not forget that there is always a close relationship between hope and listening, and Mary is a woman who listens. Mary welcomes life just as it comes to us, with its happy days but also with its tragedies that we would never have wished to encounter. Until Mary's supreme night, when her Son is nailed to the wood of the cross.

Until that day, Mary had almost disappeared from the Gospel events: the sacred writers suggest this slow overshadowing of her presence, her remaining mute before the mystery of a Son who obeys the Father. But Mary reappears just at the crucial moment: when most of his friends have run away on account of fear. Mothers do not desert, and at that moment, at the foot of the cross, none of us can say which was the crueler passion: that of an innocent man dying on a cross, or the agony of a mother who accompanies the last moments of her Son's life.

The Gospels are succinct, and extremely discreet. They record the Mother's presence with a simple verb: she was "standing by" Jesus (Jn 19:25). She stood by him. They say nothing about her reaction: if she was weeping, if she was not weeping . . . Nothing; not even a word to describe her sorrow: these details would be tackled later by the imagination of poets and painters, bestowing upon us images that have gone down in the history of art and literature. But the Gospels say only: she was "standing by" him. She stood there at the most terrible moment, at the cruelest moment, and suffered with her Son. She "stood by" him.

Mary "stood by" her Son. She simply was there. Here she is again, the young woman of Nazareth, her hair now grayed with the passing of the years, still at grips with a God who must be only embraced, and with a life that has come to the brink of the deepest darkness. Mary "stood by" him in the deepest darkness, but she "stood by" him. She did not go away. Mary is there, faithfully present, a candle kept alight in a place of mist and fog. Even she did not know the destiny of resurrection that her Son was opening at that moment for all of us: she stood there out of faithfulness to the plan of God, whose handmaid she had proclaimed herself to be on the first day of her vocation, but also because of her instinct as a mother who simply suffers every time a child undergoes a passion. The sufferings of mothers: all of us have known strong women who have faced so many sufferings of their children!

We find her there again on the first day of the Church (cf. Acts 1:14), she, the Mother of hope, in the midst of that community of disciples who were so fragile: one had denied, many had run away, all had been afraid. But she simply stood by them, in the most normal way possible, as if this were something entirely natural: in the early Church enveloped in the light of the Resurrection, but also in the trembling of the first steps it had to take in the world.

This is why we all love her as our mother. We are not orphans: we have a mother in heaven, who is the Holy Mother of God. Because she teaches us the virtue of waiting, even when everything seems meaningless: she always trusts in the mystery of God, even when he seems overshadowed by the world's evil. In times of difficulty may Mary, the Mother whom Jesus has presented as a gift to all of us, always make our steps sure; may she always say to our hearts: "Get up! Look ahead, look to the horizon," because she is the Mother of hope.

Magnificat

One of the most beautiful things, Pope Francis, is that Mary just can't wait to say goodbye to the angel and is already setting off on her journey. Speaking of faith, one of your Jesuit confreres, Saint Alberto Hurtado, used an image that fascinates me: "It is a fire that ignites other fires." And it is wonderful that the longest speech that Mary makes should be a song, the Magnificat. *And here too, yet again, Mary sings of her littleness: "My soul magnifies the Lord" (cf. Lk 1:46–47). As if to say: the merit is his, not mine. I am struck by this delving into the Word of God, this amazement at how small one is. I am reminded of that verb which has become famous thanks to your writings: "primerear." It is God who gets there first, and Mary says: "It is he who has done it, it is he who has done it." The humility of Mary . . .*

Mary takes her inspiration from the song of Hannah, Samuel's mom (cf. 1 Sam 2:1–10). She knew the Scriptures, Our Lady did, and so what came out was that marvel which was produced by her knowledge of the Scriptures but also by her capacity for amazement, joy, praise. Mary praises God, while we Christians so often forget the prayer of praise and the prayer of adoration. Mary adored God and praised God. This is what the *Magnificat* is. It comes from the desire to praise, to pray by praising God, like children who love Mom and Dad so much that they do not get tired of talking about Mom and Dad, they praise them. Lovers who love one another do not get tired of saying beautiful things about their partner to others, they praise, they praise. And praising God means getting out of oneself, something that is often difficult for our egoism.

One of Mary's forms of praise, probably also her most beautiful quality, is that of making herself available and present. I think that one of the effects of popular devotion is the phenomenon of the apparitions. And it is good to clarify something, Pope Francis. The apparitions do not

add anything to what God wanted to tell us and give us,
but I imagine them as being a bit like remedial classes:
when one is not learning a concept well, one stays after
class and explores that concept with a teacher. The appari-
tions point to Mary's dream that all should fall in love
with her Son, not so much with her. The apparitions of
Mary are a delicate page of popular faith.

Our Lady wants to take Jesus everywhere. Our Lady
did not say, in Cana, "Calm down, leave it all to me,
I'll take care of it." No, she spoke with her Son pri-
vately and then she said: "Do what he tells you" (cf.
Jn 2:5). Our Lady's finger always points to Jesus; Our
Lady never says: "I'll solve this, I have the solution."
She always points to Jesus. And the apparitions can
be spiritual experiences of the person who then passes
them on, or even a special manifestation of Our Lady
in that historical circumstance, at a time when humanity needs to hear the Gospel, to see that finger of
Mary pointing to Jesus, to hear once again: "Do what
he tells you." Yes, there are exaggerations over the
apparitions, and the Church is always very prudent.
The Church never bases the faith on apparitions. No,

the faith is rooted in the Gospel, in revelation, in the tradition of revelation. It is the Mother repeating to her children: "Think of Jesus, do what he tells you."

Is there a shrine of a Marian apparition, Pope Francis, to which you are particularly attached?

No, not particularly attached. I have a devotion to Lourdes, to Fatima, in the sense that I have respect for how Our Lady appeared. In my own country too, in Luján, Our Lady did not appear but wanted to be there with miraculous signs, with the image. In Aparecida in Brazil, she wanted to let the fishermen encounter her so that she could be the mother of Brazil, to show herself as Mother. Guadalupe says a lot to me as a [Latin] American, because in Guadalupe there is the experience of the people who go to pray to Our Lady. Or rather, they draw near so that Our Lady can look at them. Our Lady, who looks and says: "Do not be afraid. I am your mother." That experience says so much to me. The problem of the apparitions is when there are clairvoyants or those who report the apparitions and say: "Mary is like this . . ." Mary points to Jesus, but if you keep looking at Mary's finger instead of Jesus, you are not acting according to Mary's heart. It means that something in that apparition is not right.

There is an extraordinary aspect of the figure of Mary: she is also loved by some of our brothers who do not share our faith in the Son. The Muslim people, for example, are very devoted to Mary. The name of Mary is cited thirty-four times in the Quran, and I almost suspect that if one day the world returns to unity, the unity will be in the name of Mary. There is that beautiful practice, on the first day of the year, of entrusting the year to Mary. There are people who do not believe in her Son but believe in Mary. It is unusual . . .

The bishop of an African country where Christians and Muslims live in peace told me that during the year of the Jubilee of Mercy, all day long there was a line to get into the cathedral. When the people went inside, some of them lined up at the confessionals, others began to say prayers, but the majority went before the altar of Our Lady: and they were Muslims.

And the bishop asked them many times: "But why do you come here?" And they said: "The Jubilee is for us too." They went to Our Lady because Mary is close to the Muslim people.

One characteristic of Our Lady that probably matters is that of being "mediatrix." If a child were to ask: "Pope Francis, what does it mean that Mary is mediatrix," how would you explain it?

I would say that she is the one who reconciles two sides that are far apart and then goes away, she reunites and goes away. Mary never makes herself the center of attention, never. And when at the shrines or in the apparitions one sees Mary becoming the center of attention and not pointing to her Son, this does not smell right. Mary never made herself the center of attention.

And this, in fact, is also the meaning of the second part of the Magnificat, *where Mary insists on saying that he is the center of attention: he has cast down, has lifted up, has come to the help . . . And I like this humility of*

Mary. Mary does not have solutions, she offers perspectives, and in the second part of the Magnificat *it seems almost that she has recapitulated all the prophesies of the Old Testament, of Amos, of Haggai, of Isaiah, of Ezekiel, who said: "One day he will come, one day he will come . . ." And Mary says: "Here he is!" Is there a prophecy of the Old Testament that you find in the song of the* Magnificat?

As I said, there is a direct connection with the Canticle of Hannah in the first book of Samuel, which has exactly the structure of the *Magnificat*. But all the prophecies are there, and also the historical books: they sing of God who has cast down, has triumphed, has defended his people; then the prophets, Isaiah and Amos for example, when they speak of the rich and powerful—Mary says "he has humbled the powerful" (cf. Lk 1:52)—they are singing about the things of the Old Testament that the Lord has done, the great things of the Lord.

Since we have no photograph that shows us what Mary really looked like, I imagine that the most beautiful photo-

graph of Mary was taken by her Son on the Mount of the Beatitudes, when he said: "Blessed are the poor in spirit" (Mt 5:3), meaning blessed are the humble. I like to think that he had in mind the image of the mom he had seen at home. Mary's attitude of consolation reminds us that when God enters into history, he does so in order that things may not remain as they were before. So with humility I ask you, Pope Francis: where is it that you, as pope, see the sprouts of this new Kingdom that is emerging today? What are the signs of hope?

It occurs to me to use a word that I would like not to be misunderstood: "patience." When God entered the world through Mary, he entered in patience. And when I see the patient Christian people—the sick who accept their illnesses, moms of families, the elderly who are alone and tolerate being so, prisoners, the many who bear suffering with patience—I think that the one who endures with patience is united with the passion of Christ, with the passion of God in Christ. That's it, when I think of signs of hope, the word that comes to mind is precisely "patience."

I am struck by another image: Mary making the Via Crucis, but backward, from the fourteenth station to the first, seeing all the things that spoke to her of the Son who was no longer there. The word "patience" is close, etymologically, to "passion." And passion means beauty but also suffering.

Yes, one who is passionate enjoys and suffers. To enter into patience is to have the capacity to bear life's burdens on one's shoulders, but with hope, to carry them while looking forward. Only one who is impassioned is capable of patience. One who does not have the experience of Christian passion, of being impassioned, at most can become just tolerant.

There is one last question that is close to my heart. Mary experienced the first Annunciation in Nazareth, then there was the second, from the cross, when the Son says to the Mother: "Woman, behold your son." I am struck by this bond between Mary and the Church, and I am especially struck by the decision that you, Pope Francis, made with the decree Ecclesia Mater, *instituting the feast of the Blessed Virgin Mary, Mother of the Church. In what relationship do these two women stand, Mary and the Church, within the heart of Christ?*

Every year, on Monday Pentecost, we now celebrate the feast of Mary, Mother of the Church. The Church is woman, the Church is not male. We clerics are male, but we are not the Church. The Church is woman because she is bride. Mary is woman, she is Joseph's bride, fully welcoming of the Holy Spirit and therefore Mother of Christ and of the Church. This latter is the bride of Christ, temple of the Spirit, who virginally bears children for the Father in the water of baptism and with the balm of forgiveness. There is a perception of the Church's motherhood that comes from Mary's motherhood, of the Church's tenderness that comes from Mary's tenderness. I have already told the anecdote of one of my father's coworkers who was an atheist. After the war in Spain, many Republicans came to Argentina, all of them anticlerics. One of them became seriously ill. He had three children; his wife went to work too. In Buenos Aires there was (and still is) a congregation founded in France by

Fr. Étienne Pernet, Les Petites Sœurs, who took care of the sick in their own homes. The French nun (her name was Madeleine) who had gone to look after the sick man really got an earful the first few days. The man had oozing sores, and the sister, who was a nurse like all the rest of them, busied herself with taking care of him and did not respond bitterly to him. Then the man changed. The sister would go out, pick the children up from school, prepare dinner, and then go back to the convent, and when the wife came home from work everything was taken care of. After a month the man got better and thanked everyone; he had become very close to the sister. One day, as he was leaving work, one of his atheist coworkers started cursing and blaspheming when he saw two sisters walking by. The man punched him and said: "Listen, about priests and God you can say whatever you want, but leave the sisters and Our Lady alone!" So he had gotten a sense of the Church's motherhood, thanks to a sister. Therefore the women we are speaking of are not two, but three: There is Mary. There is the Church. And there is the consecrated woman. This is why the greatest glory of a sister is to be the *imago*, the icon of Mary and of the Church. The Church is female.

Pope Francis, I would like to leave with you this image of a painting that is kept at the church of Saint Augustine in Campo Marzio, in Rome. It is one of my obligatory stops. There I contemplate the Our Lady of Pilgrims *painted by Caravaggio, and I am moved by these swollen feet, these threadbare garments, these clasped hands, these reverent knees. I see myself there, and I am reminded of the prayer I have recited every evening for twenty years: "Under your protection we seek refuge, Holy Mother of God: do not despise our supplications in our distress, but deliver us from all danger, O glorious and blessed Virgin." I look at Mary, who is there on the threshold and holds her Son in her arms.*

He is more than one year old.

Why are you also bewitched by this image of Mary?

Because of its reality, its concreteness. She is a mother with a Son who is growing up in her arms, who is heavy, but she still looks at him with tenderness. She looks at these pilgrims who are passing by, who will never see her again. She looks at us when we go there. When I used to come to Rome as a bishop, I would stay just down from the Via della Scrofa, at the residence for clergy. And every morning before going to the Vatican I went to the church of Saint Augustine to visit two women, Our Lady of Pilgrims and another woman I admire a lot, Saint Monica. Monica was a real woman of the Church, a mother who knew how to be a mother like Mary and to take the cross upon herself. It moves me to see this image right now. And these pilgrims, they are us, with our life: we greet her, we tell her not to forget us, with hands clasped, supplicants. It is Our Lady of Pilgrims. And Saint Monica too—I dare to say it because I'm so fond of her—had her own *Magnificat*. When she told her son Augustine that now she could die because she had realized her desire of seeing him a Christian, she used these words: *"Cumulatius hoc mihi Deus meus praestitit."* In other words, God has given me this in abundance. It is the *Magnificat* of Monica: that church is these two women, the women who sang the *Magnificat*, each at her own level.

Pope Francis, to thank you I will recite the Hail Mary *for what is in your heart, and if you could please recite it for what is in my heart. It is our thank-you to Mary.*

Hail Mary, full of grace,

the Lord is with you.

Blessed are you among women

and blessed is the fruit of your womb, Jesus.

Holy Mary, Mother of God,

pray for us sinners,

now and at the hour of our death.

Amen.

The Joy of Faith

The [Second Vatican] Council affirms that Mary "advanced in her pilgrimage of faith" (*Lumen Gentium* 58). Because of this she precedes us on this pilgrimage, she accompanies us, she sustains us.

In what sense was Mary's faith a journey? In the sense that her whole life was a following after her Son: he, Jesus, is the way, he is the path! Moving forward in faith, advancing on this spiritual pilgrimage that is the faith, is nothing other than following Jesus; listening to him, allowing his words to guide us; seeing how he behaves and setting our feet in his footprints; having the same sentiments and attitudes. And what are they, the sentiments and attitudes of Jesus? Humility, mercy, nearness, but also the firm rejection of hypocrisy, of duplicity, of idolatry. The way of Jesus is that of love faithful to the end, to the point of sacrificing one's life; it is the way of the cross.

This is why the journey of faith passes through the cross, and Mary understood that from the start, when Herod wanted to kill Jesus right after he was born. But then this cross became even more profound, when Jesus was rejected: Mary was always with Jesus, she followed Jesus in the midst of the people, and she heard the gossip, the hatefulness of those who did not love the Lord. And this cross, she bore it! Then Mary's faith confronted incomprehension and contempt. When the "hour" of Jesus came, meaning the hour of the passion: then Mary's faith was the little flame in the night, that little flame in the middle of the night. During the night of Holy Saturday, Mary kept watch. Her flame, small but bright, stayed alight until the dawn of the Resurrection, and when she heard that the tomb was empty, her heart overflowed with the joy of faith, the Christian faith in the death and resurrection of Jesus Christ. Because faith always leads us to joy, and she is the Mother of joy: may she teach us to go by this path of joy and to live this joy! This is the summit—this joy, this encounter of Jesus and Mary, let's just imagine what it was like. This encounter is the summit of Mary's journey of faith and that of the whole Church. What is our faith like? Do we keep it alight, like Mary, even in difficult times, times of darkness? Have I felt the joy of faith? This evening, Mother, we thank you for your faith, that of a strong and humble woman; we renew our entrustment to you, Mother of our faith. Amen.

Part II

A Mother Among Wolves

by Marco Pozza

A song worms its way through the gray cement. Amid the red of the bars, the redness of the faces: *Veni creator spiritus.* The metal jar on the altar is small: inside is the oil of chrism, the oil of confirmation. Something big is about to happen. Father Michele, dressed in red, dips his thumb into the metal container. He, the young criminal, is standing right in front of him: straight and at attention, his hair electrified with gel, the hand of his catechist resting on his shoulder. A ray of light falls across his face: *"Receive the seal of the Holy Spirit given to you as a gift."* Before it happens to you, you cannot know how you will react. "Amen," he stammers. The word, once pronounced, has flown away, it cannot come back. Amen: one does not give blows without expecting, at least once, to take some. *"Peace be with you"*: the weapon of a gentleman is his kindness. God is a gentleman. The wrongdoer perceives this. He steals the words to reciprocate: *"And with your spirit."* Spoken on the fly, they are splinters of love.

The priest gives him a big hug: their expressions are unguarded, like family. Just behind him, under the protective eyes of the crew inside the prison chapel, is his mother. She is looking at everything, looking at everyone, with an expression of rapture. For years she was a mother in mourning, with a lantern in her hand, delving into the depths of the prisons to find her son. God also goes about with a lantern in hand: to look for anyone who will accept him. Who will accept the exuberance of his love. God, the mother: God is a mother. Perfumed with chrism, the young man gives his mother a big hug: all around is a forest of wolves. Glinting eyes.

He has borrowed their attention so that he can have a good cry. To cry for everything.

For her it is the final *Hail Mary*. Rung out by bells that are off-key: *"Hail Mary, full of grace."* Disgrace has become grace again. He has knocked to find it.

His story is all he has: "My name is Jacopo, I am twenty-eight and I can say with joy, without any doubt, that I am reborn." Telling stories is the main form of entertainment for criminals: they tell them in episodes, bring the details into focus, file down the edges to get them sharp. On the outside, war is waged with tanks: behind bars, it is done with rapier strokes. "When I was thirteen, social services took me from my family and put me into a foster community. I was there for three years."

The words are sullen, wary, halting. They are the echo and the memory of a childhood taken away, torn to shreds: "I was still a child. At that age I should have been playing and studying; instead I found myself dealing with drugs, alcohol, sex, and violence." His expression is intense and marked with the burden of stories that he has to either tell or go on carrying forever. "I grew up fast. At sixteen all I was learning about was the negative side: I was an expert in drugging and dealing, but I had never read a book; I was having sex but didn't know anything about love; I was surrounded by people but focused on no one but myself." Like a patron at the bar of hell.

Violence is blind, it is mute, it is deaf. The triumph of idiocy. The mere idea of doing something forbidden is pure excitement. As he talks, his spirit becomes utterly deflated. The sound is that of a glass bottle smashed to pieces. "In my life I have done the worst things a man can do: I have stolen, I have taken part in robberies, I have sold drugs, I have been an alcoholic, a drug addict." What appears on his face is the materialization of rage: a mixture of melancholy, nostalgia, pain. The important thing was to terrify: the terrified enemy is already half-defeated. "I barbarously killed a guy, and without any pity I threw him into a ditch. I wanted him to suffer right to the end, not just die." Without education, the heart withers away.

His mother, sitting in the front row, has a hard time enduring the shock of that story she brought into the world, who, for her, has remained always a child. Her ravaged eyes are vast like the Milky Way. *"The Lord is with you."* No companionship, however, in her: Lucifer, the absolutely perfectly liar, had gotten hold of her son. So much loneliness for him: "I never hated loneliness as much as when she seized hold of me down on the restraint beds and kept me prisoner, whispering in a low voice: 'You're mine, all mine.' No one else apart from her: entire days, on a bed with four straps, in her desolate company."

It appeared there was nothing but darkness: to force one to listen to her, loneliness cudgels the ears. It is a long Via Crucis: "I dedicated the next two years to brawling and bad conduct. I began to feel the weight of the shame I was causing my family, and the likelihood of a sentence too long for me to serve led me to choose the quickest way, suicide." A minor, when he is enraged, is a beast who draws blood even from his shadow. "One night I decided to end it all. I wrote a letter to my family and hung myself." To die, he had decided to become a child again: knees drawn up to his chest, eyes closed, fists clenched. Death, however, is a pampered woman. She chooses for herself which morsel to eat and which to leave: "I was saved by a cop. A little while later I found myself hospitalized in a criminal asylum." A murderer, when he is at work, knows he is being clever. When he gets to his cell, he remembers the old warnings of those who urged him to be careful.

Careful not to think he was too clever.

He was prepared to die. Since death did not come,

he had to reflect. "I spent three years in three different asylums, I felt in my flesh what it means to be tied by the ankles and wrists in a restraint bed, to be stuffed with medications. I was considered crazy, so I was marginalized." The dignity with which he tells the story is disorienting: no fear, facts at fingertips, shame on his face. His mother, praying, must have recited it too: *"Blessed are you among women."* She, instead, was cursed among women. They didn't even allow her the luxury of holding on to his name: she was the mother of the criminal, of the murderer, the shame of the city. She was no longer herself, she was the mother of her son's crime. Mother of the one who had sown chaos all over town.

The most courageous thing that a mother can do is to stay standing amid the storm. To pull her son's clothing out of the waves: *"Blessed is the fruit of your womb."* Blessing the son, when everything around is a curse, is like daring the impossible. Accepting to be trodden upon: "No fear that they may tread on me. Downtrodden, the grass becomes a path" (Blaga Dimitrova). Women stand. The male, if he does not lose his balance, hides behind the female. "After several years my father came back into my life. I began to think that for the first time things were starting to go the right way." A father who, as such, had been a disaster. A son who had been even worse. "Perhaps, for the first time, we really cared about each other. In that moment there were only a father and a son who wanted to forgive each other." In some gypsy language it was a forewarning: "He had been diagnosed with lung cancer; after a few days he died. In that moment I felt the world collapse on top of me."

Growing up without a father, with a mother as father too.

Some prisoners are like fruit left out to rot: they survive by playing cards. They play so long that they end up making it the purpose of their existence. Playing is like strolling past a masterpiece; living, instead, is like painting. No opportunity, however, makes sense without an inclination: he who loves wants the painter to paint, even if he is misunderstood. Wants him to protest with astonishment. Art is a form of protest: "One day they released me: I was no longer considered a dangerous subject. I went back to serve my sentence in prison."

The most courageous thing one can do in prison is to get up in the morning.

In the Sala Ducale of the Vatican Museums, an explosion of art and magic, there is a broad arcade concealed by an enormous drapery held up by little angels. Beneath that arcade, in a simple chair with armrests, sits Pope Francis. That place, where monarchs and heads of state pass by on official visits, is the one we have chosen for our meeting. To talk about the *Ave Maria*, about the Mother, about mothers. The mothers who are closest to his heart: "Many times while riding the bus I passed the prison of Villa Devoto in Buenos Aires. There were all the moms lined up, and everyone saw them, these women in line to get in, to visit a son." Them, always them: on last-minute getaways, with swollen feet and bags under their eyes, in the dog days of August and the January chill. Their purses, at the entrance, are like loaded washing machines: at the exit, they are like washing machines to be refilled. The clean underwear, the bread from the local bakery, the regional sausages, the homemade sauces. In prison one must never swear by one's mother: it is an unforgivable offense. They are women of conversation: in conversation when the children go to school, when the children are flung into the cold cells.

"There is a moment, during our conversations, when I go crazy: when my mother looks at me with shining eyes, then squeezes my cheek, kisses her fingers, gives me a big hug. She whispers to me: 'You are my little boy, I will love you forever.'" Mothers who are letter carriers, pro bono lawyers: they deliver, they bring back, they comfort. They are affected by amnesia: they easily forget the things that have gone wrong. But when it comes to the good things, they can cite by memory the smallest details. Francis, the pope: "It is not hard to imagine the humiliations a woman must suffer, the pat downs . . . But it doesn't matter, it's for a son. They let themselves be trodden upon." Look at them, see the Church.

They run quite a risk who smile at them as one would smile at a survivor: they never exhaust the stores of tenderness that they keep in their hearts. Forever Mom, even after the murder. Says Jacopo: "She always believed in me, she never gave up, not even when I told her: 'Let it go, it's a waste of time, it'll never change.'" She is stubborn: "Don't worry, I'm here with you. I won't send you alone into the darkness." The good will continue to try, they do not give up easily: "She found the goodness for me, it's always been like that."

There is only one remedy for shame: turning (back) to God. Appealing to his gaze of mercy: "Look to him and be radiant, and your faces may not blush for shame" (Ps 34:6). What kills is not sin: it is despair. Lucifer, the braggart, cannot stand it that evil can be forgiven.

He hates, insanely, the motherly side of God.

Prison life is a fencing match: it is important to feel the blade. "At the most difficult time of my life Jesus came in. Before then he was a guy hanging on a cross, nothing more. This morning he is a God who, with his cross, has changed me. By saving me." Playing the lowlife is always more fascinating than being well behaved: this is the criminal fascination. When the accuser loses, however, it is God who gets dressed to the nines. *Holy Mary, Mother of God.* "I just received confirmation and first communion: so far this is the most beautiful day of my life." The profession of faith, the laying on of hands, the chrismation, the universal prayer: all actions that are simple, meager, elemental. Things that vibrate with mystery do not have a spectacular appearance, they shine with paltry light. They illuminate the outlines of things, the borders of what is present: "'Today I am truly proud of you. It is absolutely the happiest day of my life.' If I think that these words, so full of love, were spoken by a mother to her own son locked up in a prison, I think that the presence of Jesus at that moment was tangible."

The mother's face is the first image of illustrated catechesis, a Jesus in cartoon. For a child, an inmate. For God. For a sinner: *"Pray for us sinners."* Sin is the death of the soul. "The soul does not stop living all of a sudden, here today and gone tomorrow, it dies slowly. Mine began to die when I was still a child. No shore on the horizon, only rocks to smash myself against." Into whatever chaos man may plunge, that will be the point of departure for going home to God: "'I have killed!' Today I understand that on that night I killed not just him, but my own soul, or what little was left of it."

At night the prison is a voracious chasm: the television shows B movies, the cigarettes are lit and extinguished at lightning speed. Words in the background stammered and carried away by the wind, the commotion of one's own thoughts, the shrieking of the demons. Remorse, mistakes, emotions faded by nicotine. The heart tormented, the head adrift: "Imagine that time never passes, that everything is motionless, that everyone else is still. But you realize that outside everything is running at an insane speed. You can't run, you can barely walk." Any problem makes the formulas worthless: the failures beg sleep to swallow them alive. At sunrise, you can hear keys out in the hallway, doors opening and closing. A new day begins, another long night has ended: "I would like to go back to when I had a soul, to when I could not imagine that one day the filth of the world would envelop me, suffocate me."

So many terrible things have happened: but he's still here.

That's no small thing.

———

The words, set down in black and white, bring up the right of reply.

My dearest son, I ask you to forgive me for not having been a good mother: maybe I could have done more. We have often talked about your behavior: only now, however, am I coming to understand some of the subtleties. I ask God to forgive me because I feel guilty, even though I thought I gave you a lot of love, so much. Guilty for not having done more so that you could grow up in a different family atmosphere. I wanted to be a special mom, but then I had to take on two roles: mother and father.

The result? I was a bull in a china shop.

Until today I have never found peace over what happened to you, I have always been a *split* mother: your mother, with so much sorrow in my heart, and the mother of the young man you killed, with infinite sorrow for that death. I will not hide it from you that your story today was for me a mountain that knocked me over: I have felt a powerful, speechless pain.

My dear son, I beg you: forgive me! I am proud of how far you have come: it is a real victory, even though it took so much effort. The Lord knows our hearts, and knows how to cleanse our sins if we turn to him with humility and sincerely ask for forgiveness. He took you by the hand, showing you his way: only by entrusting yourself to him, allowing him to embrace you, can we be reborn.

I give you a great big hug: today my embrace is even stronger. I cannot wait to see you, to be able to spend a few hours with you. I love you so much, you know: but today I say it to you in a special way. See you soon!

Mom

Years ago all hell broke loose. Thinking of defeating him then was like challenging a cheetah. But heaven knows how to wait. Heaven plans surprise attacks. It feints, backpedals, advances. It traps the enemy to make him give up. It will win, *"now and at the hour of our death."* Waiting for man to get tangled up in his freedom: "If I think of the present,

I am proud of the guy I am today, even if I sometimes wonder, 'At what price?' For much of my life I was in the company of the devil, at my side today is God. The difference? Yesterday I was dead, today I am alive. Above all, alive. I have begun to appreciate life after having taken a life. After having lost everything."

To bring a bit of order, some people need to make disorder first.

At first, after all, everything depends on us: "Ever since I came to this prison I have stopped wearing a wristwatch: I don't want to check the time anymore. Now I like to live it. The past, the present, the future: I don't know who I will be tomorrow, but I know well who I am today: I am a guy who doesn't forget who he was yesterday. And what he did yesterday."

Amen, this is how life goes in prison: one part is making mistakes, another is understanding them, and another is seeking to live without mistakes. Or at least to try.

Once again Father Michele, the man with the chrism on his thumb: *"The Mass is ended, go in peace."* In the prisons they are famous for resolving heated situations quickly. In evil, they were all people of talent. To applaud is to embrace. They are bodies that cling to each other, tempests of affection, kisses and caresses on the cheek, *"But now we must celebrate and rejoice, because your brother was dead and has come to life again; he was lost and has been found"* (Lk 15:32). They are tattooed bodies: in prison, the tattoo is a kind of identification card. Learning to interpret tattoos means guessing at the paths traveled in arriving here: one suffers, then stamps the suffering on one's flesh and tells the story for the rest of one's life. Some have tattoos on their bodies, others have tattoos with flesh wrapped around them. Jacopo also has a tattoo today: *"Receive the seal of the Holy Spirit given to you as a gift."* A seal, according to the Greek etymology, is a tattoo that is burned on: animals, slaves, soldiers. It is a mark with chrism on the forehead, with God's signature: "I am interested in you, I am not interested in your sin anymore." It is the Word of God: to give thanks to a God like this.

Tattooed embraces, reluctant tears, a storm of thoughts: *"Peace be with you."*

Pressed up against the window, the mother stares

through the grille at a long row of cells forsaken by hope. I observe her from a distance, through the eyes of her son, who studies her from within that rabble of embraces: "I have a mom and a sister who love me to pieces; it is thanks to them that I have not yet lost the will to fight." Two women, with a lantern in hand. A patience that is loyal, stubborn: "In more than nine years they have never let me feel alone. They have traveled all over Italy for me, from north to south." No criminal will ever lie to himself: "It was my fault that they experienced shame, humiliation, sorrow. They have crossed over into inhuman realities like those of prison, criminal asylums, but they never stopped loving me. On the contrary, they loved me even more." Evil, for mothers, looks like the light of the winter sun: it goes away without a lot of struggle.

It sets almost immediately.

At the door of the church, defending the boundaries, there she is: a statue of Our Lady made of wood. On their way out of Mass it is she that they look at: they give her a kiss, they make the sign of the cross, they give her (stealing it) a flower, to take it back to their cells. Some have a tattoo of her on their biceps, others wear her image on a necklace. Others in a pocket, with lettering over her crown: *"Pray for us sinners."*

Jacopo passes in front of her. He stops. On each side he holds his mother and sister by the hand. His eyes are set on her, Our Lady. The guard already has the keys in his hand: making them jingle is a warning that time is up. With time up, in here, there begins the only extra time granted: the time for a *Hail Mary*.

Looking at her is like going on vacation to rest and then coming back home.

Back to the cell.

With the perfume of a Mother still on him.

Sources

Fr. Marco Pozza's interview with Pope Francis took place in the Sala Ducale of the Vatican Museums on July 19, 2018, for TV2000.

These are the sources for the concluding passages of the sections in Part I.

The Beauty of a Woman in Whom God Dwells
Angelus for the solemnity of the Immaculate Conception of the Blessed Virgin Mary, Saint Peter's Square, December 8, 2017

Faith: Fidelity and Trust
Homily for Holy Mass on the occasion of the Marian day in the Year of Faith, part I, Saint Peter's Square, October 13, 2013

The Smile of Feeling Like Part of the People
Homily for the solemnity of Mary Most Holy, Mother of God, part II, Saint Peter's Basilica, January 1, 2017

The Maternal Tenderness of God
Homily for the solemnity of Mary Most Holy, Mother of God, part I, Saint Peter's Basilica, January 1, 2017

Act of Veneration of the Immaculate in Piazza di Spagna
Prayer to Our Lady on the occasion of the solemnity of the Immaculate Conception, Piazza di Spagna, December 8, 2013

The Lord Became Incarnate in Mary
Homily for the solemnity of Mary Most Holy, Mother of God, Saint Peter's Basilica, January 1, 2018

Undoing Knots
Catechesis on the occasion of the prayer for the Marian day in the Year of Faith, part I, Saint Peter's Square, October 12, 2013

Mother of Hope
General audience, Saint Peter's Square, May 10, 2017

The Joy of Faith
Catechesis on the occasion of the prayer for the Marian day in the Year of Faith, part III, Saint Peter's Square, October 12, 2013